my mindful day

Peace

Published in the United States of America by Cherry Lake Publishing
Ann Arbor, Michigan
www.cherrylakepublishing.com

Reading Adviser: Marla Conn, MS, Ed., Literacy specialist, Read-Ability, Inc.
Book Designer: Jennifer Wahi
Illustrator: Jeff Bane

Photo Credits: ©Syda Productions/Shutterstock, 5; ©worawit_i/Shutterstock, 7; ©Thomas M Perkins/Shutterstock, 9; ©Kamelevska Tatiana/Shutterstock, 11; ©mimagephotography/Shutterstock, 13; ©Pressmaster/Shutterstock, 15; ©atsurkan/Shutterstock, 17; ©Kateryna Omelianchenko/Shutterstock, 19; ©anek.soowannaphoom/Shutterstock, 21; ©Sergey Novikov/Shutterstock, 23; Cover, 8, 10, 16, Jeff Bane; Various vector images throughout courtesy of Shutterstock.com

Library of Congress Cataloging-in-Publication Data has been filed and is available at catalog.loc.gov

Printed in the United States of America
Corporate Graphics

table of contents

About the author: Katie Marsico is the author of more than 200 reference books for children and young adults. She lives with her husband and six children near Chicago, Illinois.

About the illustrator: Jeff Bane and his two business partners own a studio along the American River in Folsom, California, home of the 1849 Gold Rush. When Jeff's not sketching or illustrating for clients, he's either swimming or kayaking in the river to relax.

Is life ever too loud?

Phones ring.

Computers beep.

Stress is noisy too.

Worries echo in our mind.

They keep us from being calm.

They make it hard to **focus**.

When do you have trouble focusing?

Stress is part of our world.

So is noise.

Yet peace is possible.

We create our own calm.

What does **inner peace** do?

It doesn’t make stress go away.

But it helps us stay happy.

Inner peace changes our view of life.

It makes us more positive.

Peaceful people are calm.

They see the best in a **situation**.

When was a time you were positive?

Staying calm isn’t always easy.

We’re used to busy, noisy lives.

Our thoughts and feelings get rushed.

Calming down means slowing down.

We must be **mindful** of this moment.

Finding inner peace takes practice!

Some people **meditate**.

Yoga also helps.

These exercises are calming.

We need to be aware of how we treat others.

It's best to be honest about feelings.

This helps us deal with **conflict**.

This helps give us inner peace.

Problems happen.

They're part of life.

Yet they're not everything.

Inner peace lets us see the bigger picture.

How can you be mindful today?

glossary & index

glossary

conflict (KAHN-flikt) a fight or struggle

focus (FOH-kuhs) to give your attention to

inner peace (IN-ur PEES) a quiet and calm state of mind

meditate (MED-ih-tate) to train your mind to relax and focus

mindful (MINDE-ful) aware of your body, mind, and feelings

situation (sich-oo-AY-shuhn) the facts that exist at a certain time and place

stress (STRES) worry that weighs heavily on your mind

yoga (YOH-guh) poses, breathing, and sometimes meditation and chanting that provide balance and good health

index